# Contents

▼ **INTRODUCTION**

4  One world: spaceship Earth

▼ **THE LIVING WORLD**

6  Why living things become extinct
8  Endangered elephants and whales
10  The many threats to all animals
12  Endangering our forests
14  Return of the wilderness
16  A garden for all
18  Better ways to farm land
20  It's easy to destroy a river

▼ **USING RESOURCES WISELY**

22  We can't help consuming
24  When we turn on a light
26  Saving energy at home
28  Saving energy, land and trees
30  Saving water

▼ **MANAGING OUR WASTE**

32  The waste we create
34  What can we do with plastics?
36  Making use of paper
38  Environmentally friendly materials

▼ **CLEANING UP AFTER OURSELVES**

40  Water pollution
42  Oil pollution
44  Air pollution

▼ **REFERENCE**

46  Glossary
48  Index

**Glossary words** 363.7

There is a glossary on pages 46–47. Glossary terms
are referred to in the text by using CAPITALS.

Big game hunting

# One world: spaceship Earth

**Of all the living things that have existed on the Earth, we are the only ones that have ever been able to change the world.**

We are living things. But we are just one kind, or **SPECIES**, of living thing. There are millions of other kinds of living things on this small planet, spaceship Earth (picture ①).

## Why do we change things?

Most living things need food, air and water. Our need for food makes us plough the land and keep cows, sheep and chickens. It makes us cut down forests and replace them with pastures and crops. It makes us fish in the world's great oceans. Our need for water makes us build dams, flood valleys and do many other things that cause damage.

We also need to keep warm and be comfortable. For this we dig coal and drill for oil, get metals from rocks, make electricity, run cars and build homes. Above all, we make machines, and with them we change the world.

▶ ① It is easier to remember that we are on a spaceship if we see the world from outside.

▲ ② We have the ability to destroy – AIR POLLUTION mixes with rain to produce ACID RAIN. Water pollution gets into rivers and lakes. This can kill trees and animals such as fish, as well as harming the health of ourselves.

## What change has caused

The way we can change the world around us has given us wonderful opportunities to make our lives better, but it has come at a price. Our wastes have also **POLLUTED** the land, the water and the air (picture ②). We have also affected all of the living things that share the Earth with us. Some have been helped by us, but many more have suffered.

▲ ③ We can protect our environment as neighbours in
our local community, such as looking after this pond.

## Our responsibilities

Every living thing has its own ideal
home, or **HABITAT**. All living things
– including ourselves – depend on
the other living things around it.

Because we have such power to
destroy, we have a duty to be
sensitive to other living things.
This is called **STEWARDSHIP**
(pictures ③ and ④).

In this book we shall see
that, if we are going to look
after – **CONSERVE** – our world
and not damage it or pollute
it more than we can help, we
have to know what we are doing
wrong and how to work in a
way that is friendly to the world
around us.

It is a big task, so turn the pages
to find out some of the things that we
do wrong and how we might tackle
our problems.

◀▼ ④ The government can
take powers to set land aside
and protect it, giving land for
wildlife and places where we
can walk.

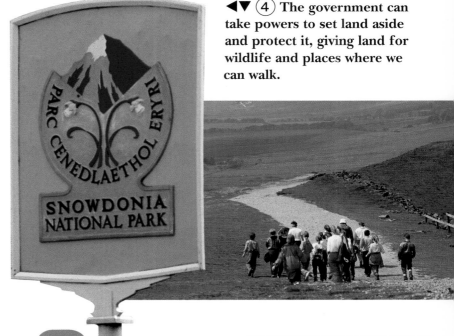

5

# Why living things become extinct

**Although there are countless living things in the world, each one has to look after itself, find its own home and adapt to the world around it. Some have been lost by natural causes – others, however, have suffered at our hands.**

The dinosaurs are some of the biggest creatures that ever lived on land (picture ①). They survived for hundreds of millions of years and then, about 65 million years ago they died out – they became **EXTINCT** – due to natural causes.

## Natural events

Over 90% of all the species that ever lived in the world are now extinct as a result of natural causes. We only know of them because their remains are preserved in rocks as **FOSSILS**.

▲ ① Dinosaurs went extinct naturally. We can only guess at what they looked like by making reconstructions from their bones. This is *Tyrannosaurus rex*, one of the largest land animals ever to have existed.

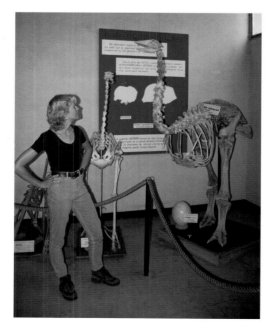

▶ ② The extinct elephant bird of Madagascar was one of the largest birds to have walked the planet. It was probably even bigger than the Moa of New Zealand. It was wiped out by the people who lived in Madagascar at the end of the 19th century.

## The impact of people

Today, the number of species going extinct is far greater than at almost any time, except for the most catastrophic of natural causes. Today's extinctions are due to people (picture ②).

When people cut down forests, grow crops and build cities they change the **BALANCE OF NATURE**. Many kinds of living things find themselves without food or a place to live.

## The sad history of the dodo

In 1598, Portuguese sailors arrived on the island of Mauritius in the southern Indian Ocean and were amazed to find a very large grey, flightless bird, like a chicken with a huge hooked bill (picture ③). The bird showed no signs of being afraid of the sailors and so they called it the dodo – meaning 'silly' – because they could not understand why the bird did not run away.

The dodo did not run away because it had no natural enemies on the island – until the sailors arrived.

In fact, although the sailors killed some of the dodos, they were not to be its main enemy. Along with the sailors came dogs and pigs.

The dodo, being flightless, nested on the ground. As a result, both its eggs and its young were at the mercy of the pigs and dogs.

By 1681 the dodo was extinct. We do not even have any reliable portraits of it, as many of the pictures were painted by people who had never seen the bird.

The dodo is a classic example of how people can, often without knowing it, so upset the balance of nature that other living things become extinct.

This was the tragedy of the dodo, for it lived in balance with all the other living things around it. A few years after the dodo was exterminated, the seeds of the calvaria tree no longer sprouted in as many places as before. This was because the seeds used to sprout after they had been eaten by the dodo as part of its food. So the death of one animal led to a decline in numbers of a plant.

Although all of this happened three centuries ago, the world lost a unique bird. It is still useful as a symbol of how people can and do cause destruction.

▲ ③ What the dodo might have looked like.

7

# Endangered elephants and whales

**Some people think of animals as something just waiting to be used up. This has had disastrous effects on elephants and whales.**

When the numbers of an animal or plant species get very small, they are called **ENDANGERED**. Both the elephant and the whale are endangered.

Some large animals can be a source of valuable meat, oil or bone. Elephants and whales have both suffered in this way. Elephants because they are the source of tusk ivory, whales because they are a source of meat and oil.

▲ ① An African bull elephant with massive tusks of ivory.

▼ ② Animals can become endangered if they are valuable. People hunt elephants just for the ivory of their tusks – they then leave the rest of the animal to rot. Here you can see the ivory tusks and the skins and heads of many other animals. This picture of hunting trophies was taken in the early 20th century.

▲ ③ Ivory is seen as precious and is used for jewellery, ornaments and other highly prized decorations. Rhinoceros horns are also seen by some people as a potent drug. The demand for ivory and rhino horn has been an important factor in creating an incentive for poaching of elephants and rhinos.

▼ ④ Slaughtering whales.

## Elephants

The African elephant is the largest land animal in the world. It weighs up to 6 tonnes and can be over 3 m high at the shoulder (picture ①). The Asian elephant is slightly smaller but still weighs over 2 tonnes.

For centuries, local people hunted the elephants for food, but this had little effect on their numbers because the numbers they killed were small.

When people arrived with guns, huge numbers were killed just for their tusks (picture ②). Ivory is still highly valued (picture ③) and although it is illegal to trade in ivory, **POACHERS** continue to kill even elephants protected in national parks.

The numbers of African and Asian elephants have been cut in half in the last three generations due to poaching. That is, there are only half as many elephants in the world as there were 60 years ago. If this continues, elephants will soon be extinct. This is why they are endangered.

## Whales

Whales are the largest animal in the whole world. But several species of whale, including the right whale and the blue whale were hunted almost to extinction for their oil, meat and 'whalebone' (picture ④).

It is a long time since people needed to kill whales for meat or oil. Despite attempts to ban whale hunting, some countries continue to kill these beautiful creatures today.

# The many threats to all animals

**We are making things more and more difficult for many living things.**

We share much with all living things. We need food to live, air to breathe and water to drink. We also need to protect ourselves from those that would harm us.

## Killing off our competitors

Humans are among the most successful living things on the planet. But our success means that other living things have often suffered.

This is because, as people farm land and make life better for themselves, they have taken away space and food used by other living things.

Some changes that would take place very slowly, and some that would not take place at all, happen quickly because of the activities of people.

## Meat-eaters suffer most

It is often the large hunting animals, the **CARNIVORES**, that have suffered most (pictures ① and ②).

People do not want to see their farm animals eaten by a lion, a puma, a wild cat or a fox. They fear, sometimes unjustly, that they are threatened by a pack of wolves, or by bears and coyotes. Some people think it is right to kill all of these animals.

◀ ① The 'common wolf' was hunted because its natural food – grazing animals – is the same as that of people. People began to call it the "big, bad, wolf".

▼ ② There are probably less than 500 Ethiopian wolves left in the world, making them amongst the rarest animals on the planet. Without protection they may well become extinct in the next 20 years.

## Conserving in a wilderness

One answer lies in giving hunting animals their own space (picture ③) This is more easily done in large countries and continents, and in places where people do not want to live.

Areas of the remote Rocky Mountains in North America, for example, have been set aside to remain undisturbed **WILDERNESS**. These areas are called national parks. In these places, animals such as wolves and bears have been reintroduced.

## Conserving in a game park

In other parts of the world, such as Africa and Asia, there are few areas where people do not go. Big cats like the lion can be dangerous to people, so how can they be helped to survive?

One way is to make large **GAME PARKS** which are used to attract tourists. The money from the tourists goes back to the local area, and so people make money from the land just as they would from other activities, like farming.

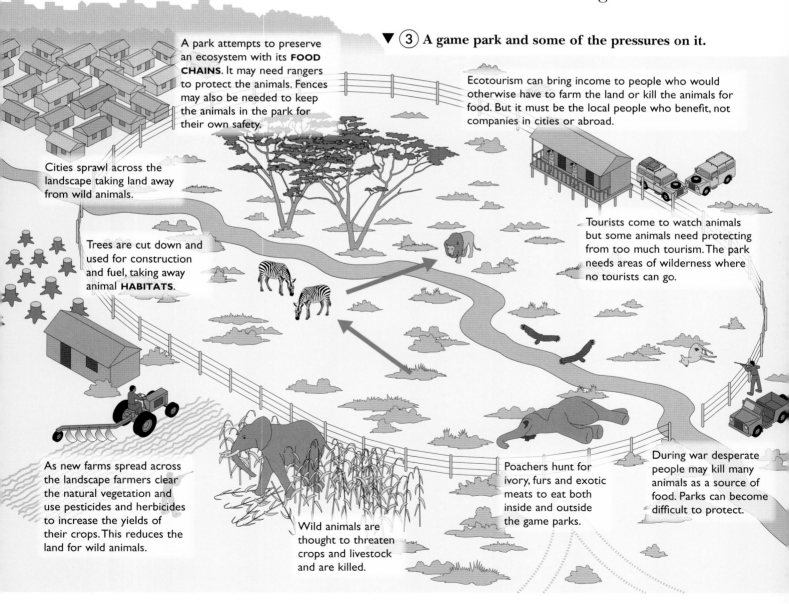

▼ ③ **A game park and some of the pressures on it.**

A park attempts to preserve an ecosystem with its **FOOD CHAINS**. It may need rangers to protect the animals. Fences may also be needed to keep the animals in the park for their own safety.

Cities sprawl across the landscape taking land away from wild animals.

Trees are cut down and used for construction and fuel, taking away animal **HABITATS**.

As new farms spread across the landscape farmers clear the natural vegetation and use pesticides and herbicides to increase the yields of their crops. This reduces the land for wild animals.

Wild animals are thought to threaten crops and livestock and are killed.

Ecotourism can bring income to people who would otherwise have to farm the land or kill the animals for food. But it must be the local people who benefit, not companies in cities or abroad.

Tourists come to watch animals but some animals need protecting from too much tourism. The park needs areas of wilderness where no tourists can go.

Poachers hunt for ivory, furs and exotic meats to eat both inside and outside the game parks.

During war desperate people may kill many animals as a source of food. Parks can become difficult to protect.

**11**

# Endangering our forests

**Many plants become endangered as we change our forests.**

▼ ① The Caledonian Forest, which was made mostly of Scots Pine trees, once extended over the whole of the highlands of Scotland. But some forest land has been used for farming, and much cut down and replanted with trees that do not naturally grow in Scotland. Yet it is still one of the most extensive forested areas in the UK. Here are some of the animals and plants you might see in it.

Flocks of cross-bills, with their specially adapted beaks, feed on pine cone seeds.

Scots Pine is dominant but birch is also common

Crested tits scour the needles and twigs for insects.

Long-eared owls prey on small mice, shrews and voles.

Pine martens hunt small animals but will also take nest eggs.

Horntails (a large sawfly) lay their eggs in pine trunks. Their larva feed on the wood.

Red deer graze and shelter in the woodland.

Red squirrels feed on pine cones and fruit from the forest floor. They help new trees by burying winter stores of seeds and forgetting where some lie.

Wood ants break down needles and other dead plant matter.

Trunk of fallen tree provides food for beetles, woodlice and millipedes.

Below the pines are heather, bracken, bilberry and carpets of moss. More unusual plants include creeping lady's tresses orchids.

The large grouse-like capercaille is found in mature forests.

Wildcat hunts at night and rests hidden during the day.

If you walk through a natural forest you may not see many living things, but they are there (picture ①). Some are simply keeping out of your way, some only move about at night, while others are too small to see easily.

## The need for wood

We need wood for many things: to make the paper of this book, for the planks on the floor of a house, and so on. The question is: how do we get wood without upsetting the environment?

## Plantations

If you cut down a natural forest, with all of its varied trees and wildlife, and replace it with just one kind of tree, planted in rows, you have made a farm of trees, which is called a **PLANTATION** (pictures ②, ③ and ④).

The naturally varied spacing of trees is replaced by trees planted to be so close together their branches have no chance of growing.

▲ ② The Cairngorms. In the foreground are two Scots Pine trees. The upper mountain slopes have had their forests cut down, while the lower slopes are replanted with conifers.

▲ ③ A dense planting of spruce trees.

The forest is tidy for efficient harvesting and so few fallen trunks and branches are available for insects that would be food for other animals.

The tough, waxy pine needles decay slowly in the cold, dark interior of the forest. They accumulate, making it difficult for plants to grow below the trees.

## Decreasing forests

Trees and forests are vital to life on our planet. They produce oxygen, store carbon, provide homes for wildlife, and provide us with raw materials and shelter.

At the end of the ICE AGE, woodland covered almost all of Britain – even the mountains. Now natural ancient forests cover only 2% of the land. Most ancient woodland still has no legal protection.

Even including plantations, forests now cover just an eighth of the land.

We have only three native conifer species and 29 broadleaved tree species.

Most plantations are conifers, and most of these are trees that do not naturally grow here.

Because conifers grow faster than broadleaved trees, plantation owners can get their money back faster. As a result, in 1980 only 5% of the trees planted were broadleaved. But now, thanks to better policies, 40% of new plantings are of broadleaved trees.

◀ ④ Plantations cast a particularly dark shade which stops many other plants from growing. The forest floor has mosses but little else. Thinning plantations would let more light in, but adding other kinds of trees and spacing trees more widely would allow even more species to thrive.

This gives straight trees that are easy to cut. But it is a silent world without bird song and with few other animals.

When trees die naturally in a forest, their leaves and trunks rot and the nourishment they contained seeps back into the soil and is used as food by the next generation of trees. Trees that are harvested and taken to sawmills cannot return anything to the soil. So plantations take nutrients and do not give them back.

The soil becomes less and less **FERTILE** and eventually even newly planted trees will not grow well.

# Return of the wilderness

**Cutting down the wilderness takes just five days. Putting back the wilderness can take 50 years.**

Gradually, over many centuries, we have destroyed much of our natural forest. The land is now used for farms, planted forests, factories, quarries, roads and cities.

It is easy to destroy a natural environment (picture ①). You wait until it is dry then burn it down. This is how the British removed the trees two thousand years ago, how the Americans cleared land two centuries ago (picture ②) and how many people in Brazil are clearing the Amazon rainforest today. It requires no tools, no skill, just a flame.

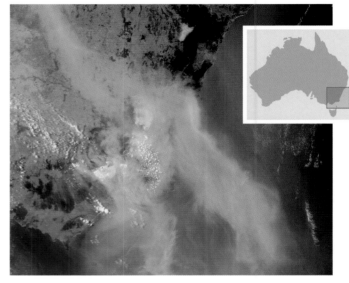

▲ ① **Careless dropping of lighted matches or cigarettes causes immense damage to the Australian forests each year. Large areas are destroyed in days, but the trees take decades to regrow. This picture of a fire was taken from a satellite and shows giant smoke trails stretching out over the ocean.**

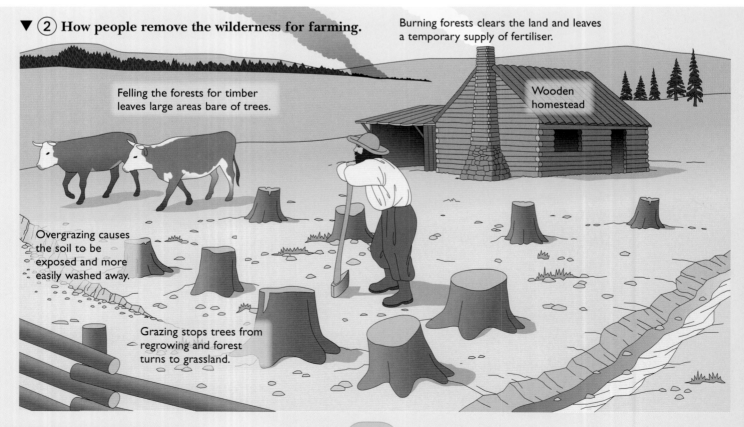

▼ ② **How people remove the wilderness for farming.**

Burning forests clears the land and leaves a temporary supply of fertiliser.

Felling the forests for timber leaves large areas bare of trees.

Wooden homestead

Overgrazing causes the soil to be exposed and more easily washed away.

Grazing stops trees from regrowing and forest turns to grassland.

▶ ③ What the Shenandoah National Park looks like today.

## You can turn farmland back to wilderness

We have many areas of spoiled and unused land. But we can turn many of them back to wilderness.

We can turn quarries back into lakes surrounded by country parks. But we can do this on a bigger scale, too. In the United States, a whole section of the Appalachian Mountains was bought from farmers who were misusing the land. It was then made into a national park and allowed to regrow naturally (pictures ③ and ④). It has taken 70 years so far, but a natural balance of plants and animals has just about returned.

▼ ④ By patient rebuilding and mostly leaving nature alone, farmland can be restored to wilderness, as shown here in this example from America.

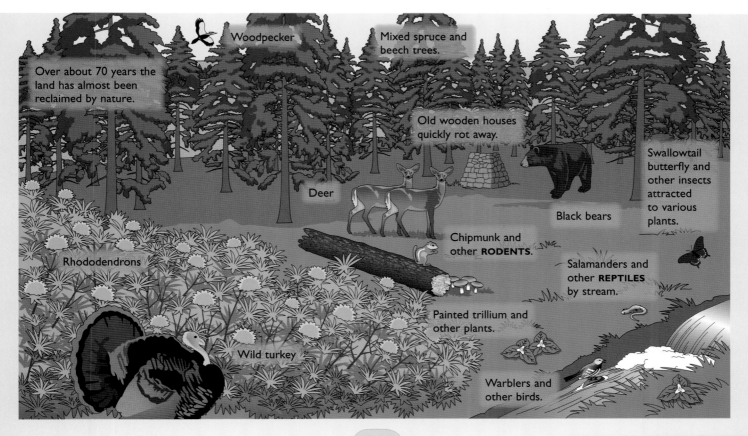

Over about 70 years the land has almost been reclaimed by nature.

Woodpecker

Mixed spruce and beech trees.

Old wooden houses quickly rot away.

Swallowtail butterfly and other insects attracted to various plants.

Deer

Black bears

Chipmunk and other **RODENTS**.

Salamanders and other **REPTILES** by stream.

Rhododendrons

Painted trillium and other plants.

Wild turkey

Warblers and other birds.

# A garden for all

**If you have a garden, then you can take a step towards improving the environment for other living things as well as yourself.**

Wherever you are, the land you now live on was once wilderness. By building homes, we take from the countryside. What was once a place of variety becomes just a lawn and a fence. But it need not be that way.

## What is a garden for?

We each have our own view of what a garden is for. To some people it may be a place to pave over and keep a car, to others a place to have a lawn.

Whether we use a garden as a place to play, to exercise the dog or as a place to grow lots of colourful flowers, we can all ask the same question: "Do we need to use it for just one purpose, or can we share it with other living things?" (picture ①).

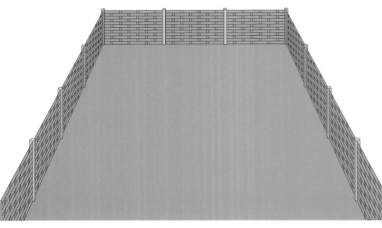

◀▼ ① **Just look at the difference between a bare garden with only grass, and a garden planted to give variety for plants and animals.**

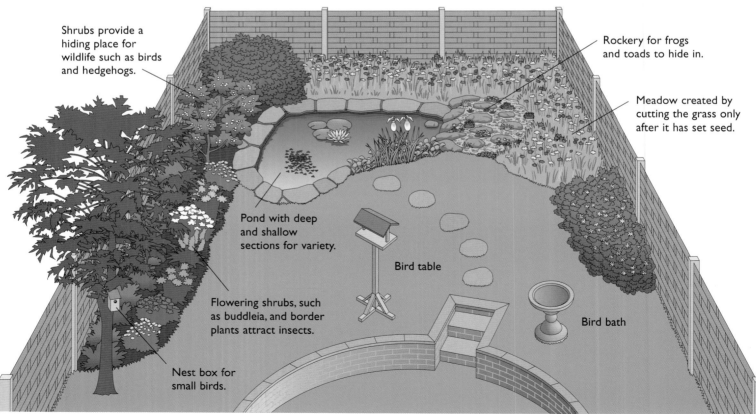

Shrubs provide a hiding place for wildlife such as birds and hedgehogs.

Rockery for frogs and toads to hide in.

Meadow created by cutting the grass only after it has set seed.

Pond with deep and shallow sections for variety.

Bird table

Flowering shrubs, such as buddleia, and border plants attract insects.

Bird bath

Nest box for small birds.

▼ ② A garden border and hedge that is friendly to wildlife and pretty to look at.

Trees provide homes for birds, insects and squirrels.

Fields

Shrubs are sheltered feeding perches for many birds.

Small **MAMMALS** such as voles can be found here.

**HERBACEOUS PLANTS** provide seeds and pollen for birds and insects, including butterflies. Some can be **ANNUALS**; the larger ones can be **PERENNIALS**.

## A hedge, not a fence

We could start by looking at the edge of the garden (picture ②). This is the part we use least. A wooden fence gives no place for other living things.

On the other hand, a **HEDGE** provides a place for many small living things to thrive. Insects will come for the **POLLEN** in the flowers and birds will find shelter and nesting sites. But if you can't have a hedge, even a climbing plant fixed to a fence will make a home for many small animals.

## Attractive shrubs

**SHRUBS** are woody plants that do not grow as large as trees. They last for many years and need very little attention. On the other hand, they help give shelter and food to animals and shade for other plants that do not like bright sunshine.

## Room for a tree?

Do you have room for a tree? Even a small garden can have a small tree. A tree provides shade and a place to plant spring bulbs. If you plant a tree near the edge and at the back of your garden, it will look good and not take up much space. If it is close to a neighbour's tree then the 'mini-forest' you create will give many more places for birds and other animals to live.

# Better ways to farm land

**To be successful at farming, must we go against the natural laws of a balanced community? Or are there ways we can work with nature?**

Food is the most basic of our needs. Without it we starve and die. The more of us there are, the more food we need to produce.

## From natural to managed land

As we have seen in the first part of this book, a balanced community contains many kinds of living things.

A farmer's job is to grow food. Because we can only eat some animals and plants, farmers cannot keep a balanced community. For example, many fields grow only **CEREAL** crops such as wheat, maize and rice. Other fields only have grass because this is food for animals such as cattle, sheep and pigs.

## The dangers in harvesting

A natural environment **RECYCLES** its nourishment. Plants that die release nourishment for new plants in the same place.

But farmers often take everything away from the fields at harvest time and leave nothing to be recycled. In time, this will lead to soils becoming poorer and poorer.

It is important to link patches of woodland with corridors made from hedges. This allows wildlife to move about more safely.

Setting aside field edges to grow naturally can create a great deal of variety. Ponds dug out of waterlogged soils in the corners of fields provide a habitat for birds such as lapwings and moorhens, as well as frogs and many insects.

Main roads make it dangerous and difficult for animals such as deer, badger and fox to move about safely. Wide bridges planted with vegetation provide a safe corridor above the traffic – and they can be used by farm vehicles, too.

Ploughing back the stubble after harvest, rather than burning it off, is one way to help put nourishment back into the soil.

The waste from cattle kept on farms is used to fertilise the crops. (But too much fertiliser will pollute water supplies, so care is needed).

## Organic farming

**ORGANIC FARMING** is one way of working with nature and at the same time getting enough food for our needs (picture ①).

The first rule is to make sure the soil gets enough nourishment. Without it, new crops will not grow.

One way to do this is to plough in the unwanted plant remains after harvest, or add animal manure. The rotted material releases nourishment and completes a natural cycle.

▼ ① **Farming and land use that is designed to be friendly to all living things.**

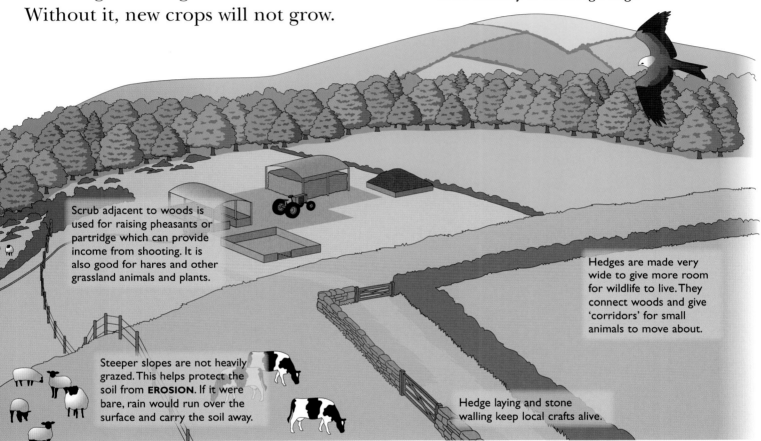

Scrub adjacent to woods is used for raising pheasants or partridge which can provide income from shooting. It is also good for hares and other grassland animals and plants.

Hedges are made very wide to give more room for wildlife to live. They connect woods and give 'corridors' for small animals to move about.

Steeper slopes are not heavily grazed. This helps protect the soil from **EROSION**. If it were bare, rain would run over the surface and carry the soil away.

Hedge laying and stone walling keep local crafts alive.

## Organic pest and weed control

**PESTS** are animals that live in fields and eat the same food as us. They often also spoil it in the process.

One way to keep soil pests under control without using chemicals is to grow a different type of crop in the soil each year. All pests are food for natural hunters, so making sure that the environment is suited to the hunters will make sure the pests are also kept under control.

**WEEDS** are wild plants that grow up with the plants we sow. To keep them down, the land can be hoed, a layer of rotting plants (called a **MULCH**) laid, or the food crops can be planted so close together that they shade out any weeds.

# It's easy to destroy a river

**You can't know the damage you are doing unless you understand how all living things depend on one another.**

We often take our environment for granted and never realise how much change – and damage – has occurred. For example, how natural are the rivers near to where you live, and how much wildlife still lives in them and near them?

## Is it natural?

Next time you look at a river, ask yourself if it looks natural or altered by people. For example, picture ① shows a river with grassy banks and ducks. You may think everything is fine. But this is only because you have got so used to this kind of riverside. In fact, it is an example of poor **STEWARDSHIP**.

## Is it polluted?

Rivers must not only look clean, they must be clean. Many materials we put in rivers cause pollution and kill plants and animals (picture ③).

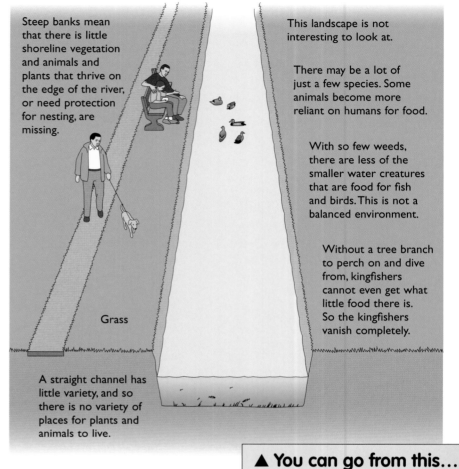

▼ ① A straightened river with little natural life.

Steep banks mean that there is little shoreline vegetation and animals and plants that thrive on the edge of the river, or need protection for nesting, are missing.

This landscape is not interesting to look at.

There may be a lot of just a few species. Some animals become more reliant on humans for food.

With so few weeds, there are less of the smaller water creatures that are food for fish and birds. This is not a balanced environment.

Without a tree branch to perch on and dive from, kingfishers cannot even get what little food there is. So the kingfishers vanish completely.

Grass

A straight channel has little variety, and so there is no variety of places for plants and animals to live.

**▲ You can go from this...**

## Natural variety

Now look at picture ② and see what could be living in the same place!

In the river there are now fast-flowing areas and slow-flowing stretches; there are shallow places and deep pools; there are open and shaded areas. All of this variety gives many more species a chance to thrive than in an altered river.

▼ ② **A natural river teeming with wildlife.**

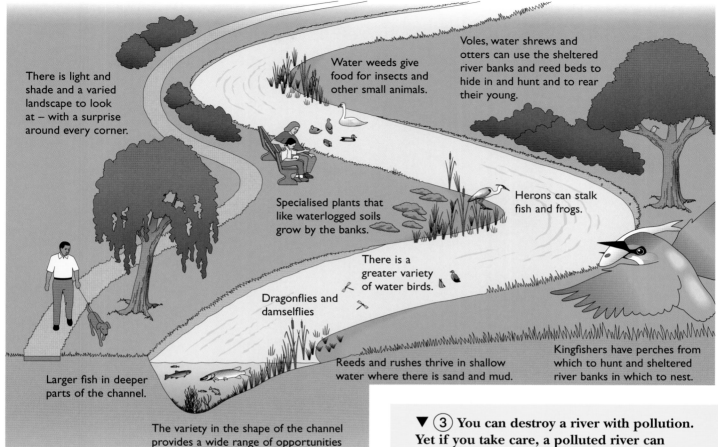

There is light and shade and a varied landscape to look at – with a surprise around every corner.

Water weeds give food for insects and other small animals.

Voles, water shrews and otters can use the sheltered river banks and reed beds to hide in and hunt and to rear their young.

Specialised plants that like waterlogged soils grow by the banks.

Herons can stalk fish and frogs.

There is a greater variety of water birds.

Dragonflies and damselflies

Larger fish in deeper parts of the channel.

Reeds and rushes thrive in shallow water where there is sand and mud.

Kingfishers have perches from which to hunt and sheltered river banks in which to nest.

The variety in the shape of the channel provides a wide range of opportunities for living things to thrive.

**...to this, with just a little care and thought. ▲**

Look back at picture ① and you may now see it in a different way. Notice, for example, how few dead leaves reach the river bed for insects and other creatures to eat. As a result, there is not much insect food for fish or tadpoles. This means there are only small numbers of fish for birds, such as herons and kingfishers, to eat and so not many of them can thrive.

As you can see, it is easy to destroy a river, but it is also easy to make a river more natural again.

▼ ③ **You can destroy a river with pollution. Yet if you take care, a polluted river can recover. In 1957 the River Thames was too polluted for any fish, but see what had happened by 1987, as the river was cleaned up.**

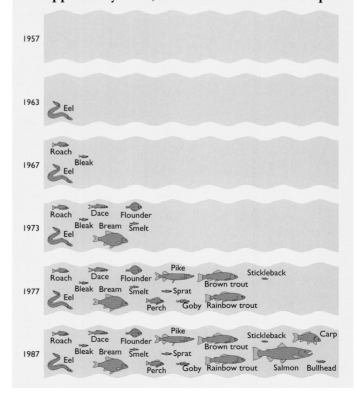

1957

1963 — Eel

1967 — Roach, Bleak, Eel

1973 — Roach, Dace, Flounder, Bleak, Bream, Smelt, Eel

1977 — Roach, Dace, Flounder, Pike, Stickleback, Bleak, Bream, Smelt, Sprat, Brown trout, Eel, Perch, Goby, Rainbow trout

1987 — Roach, Dace, Flounder, Pike, Stickleback, Carp, Bleak, Bream, Smelt, Sprat, Brown trout, Eel, Perch, Goby, Rainbow trout, Salmon, Bullhead

# We can't help consuming

**As we go about our daily lives, we use all kinds of resources. Most of the time we don't even think about them and this is why disasters happen.**

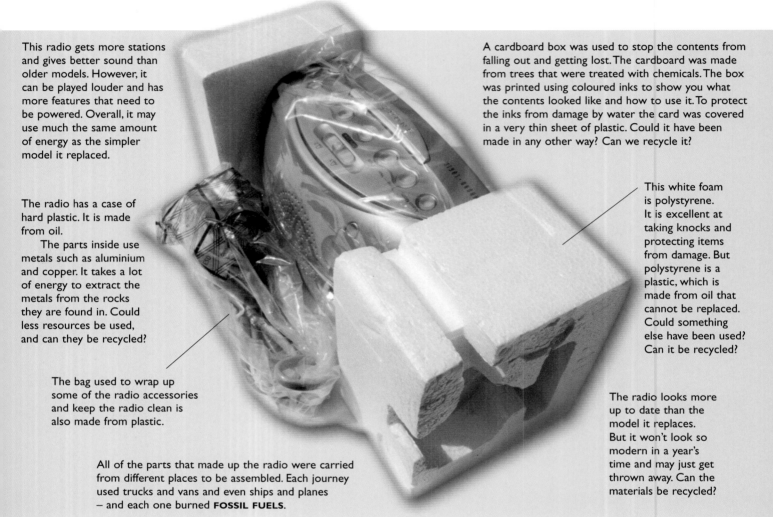

This radio gets more stations and gives better sound than older models. However, it can be played louder and has more features that need to be powered. Overall, it may use much the same amount of energy as the simpler model it replaced.

The radio has a case of hard plastic. It is made from oil.
 The parts inside use metals such as aluminium and copper. It takes a lot of energy to extract the metals from the rocks they are found in. Could less resources be used, and can they be recycled?

The bag used to wrap up some of the radio accessories and keep the radio clean is also made from plastic.

All of the parts that made up the radio were carried from different places to be assembled. Each journey used trucks and vans and even ships and planes — and each one burned **FOSSIL FUELS**.

A cardboard box was used to stop the contents from falling out and getting lost. The cardboard was made from trees that were treated with chemicals. The box was printed using coloured inks to show you what the contents looked like and how to use it. To protect the inks from damage by water the card was covered in a very thin sheet of plastic. Could it have been made in any other way? Can we recycle it?

This white foam is polystyrene. It is excellent at taking knocks and protecting items from damage. But polystyrene is a plastic, which is made from oil that cannot be replaced. Could something else have been used? Can it be recycled?

The radio looks more up to date than the model it replaces. But it won't look so modern in a year's time and may just get thrown away. Can the materials be recycled?

▲ ① **This radio looks harmless enough. It would be very useful. But do you need to replace an old one quite so often?**
 **This may seem like a silly question until you stop to think about your actions. Look to see how connected this small item is to the world around you.**

We are living things with a difference. Unlike other living things, we have the ability to change the world around us.

## Using up resources

Everything that we make use of is called a **RESOURCE**. It may be wood from trees, electricity from coal, petrol from oil or clay from the ground.

When we use a resource we **CONSUME** it. We cannot help but be consumers, but we can choose to be thoughtless or thoughtful consumers.
 If we are thoughtless consumers, we waste the precious resources of the Earth. We destroy the land for

other living things, and leave the land polluted and covered in waste. In this way we can cause disasters and leave the land poorer for the generations that follow.

If we are thoughtful, we can still have good lives, but we affect the world less and leave it in better shape for generations that follow. You can think about this as you look at the examples here and on the following pages.

▼ ② **Houses are big consumers of materials, although we tend not to think about them in this way.**

## Buying goods

All goods are made of materials (picture ①), but have the goods been made with recycling in mind? Have they been designed to use the smallest amount of materials?

## Living at home

Houses are made of materials, too (picture ②). Have they been made with recycled materials, with materials that do not harm the landscape, or do they use precious materials that cannot be replaced?

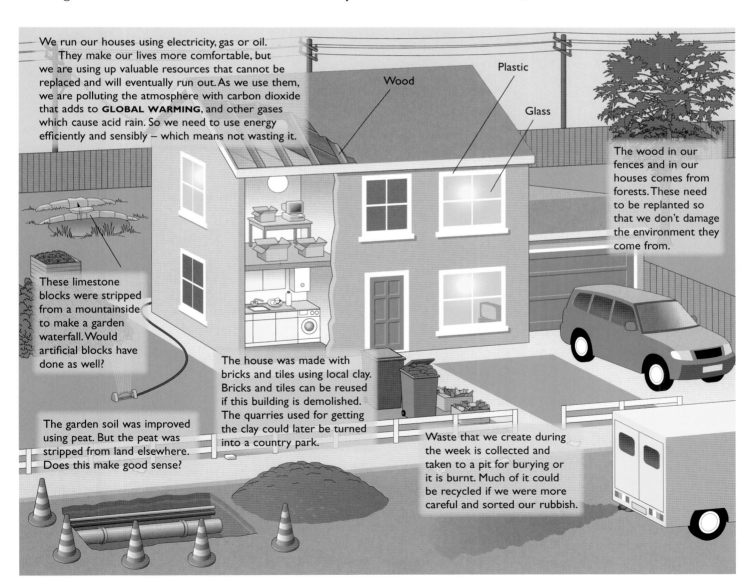

We run our houses using electricity, gas or oil. They make our lives more comfortable, but we are using up valuable resources that cannot be replaced and will eventually run out. As we use them, we are polluting the atmosphere with carbon dioxide that adds to **GLOBAL WARMING**, and other gases which cause acid rain. So we need to use energy efficiently and sensibly – which means not wasting it.

Wood

Plastic

Glass

The wood in our fences and in our houses comes from forests. These need to be replanted so that we don't damage the environment they come from.

These limestone blocks were stripped from a mountainside to make a garden waterfall. Would artificial blocks have done as well?

The house was made with bricks and tiles using local clay. Bricks and tiles can be reused if this building is demolished. The quarries used for getting the clay could later be turned into a country park.

The garden soil was improved using peat. But the peat was stripped from land elsewhere. Does this make good sense?

Waste that we create during the week is collected and taken to a pit for burying or it is burnt. Much of it could be recycled if we were more careful and sorted our rubbish.

# When we turn on a light

**A simple action such as turning on a light can't have any impact, can it? Yes it can, when billions of people do this and other similar things every day.**

I don't use much of the world's resources, do you? Your answer is probably the same as mine. None of us think we use much. But there are so many of us now that together we make a big difference – and often in ways we may not even dream about (picture ①).

## Switch on

To see how we have an impact, let's look at a light bulb, something we use every day.

The glass, metal and plastic for the bulb have to come from the ground (glass from sand, metal from rocks, plastic from oil). So the more times we change the bulb, the more of these resources we use up.

The bulb has to be made by machines. These are made of resources, too, and they need energy to run them.

The bulb needs energy – in the form of electricity. When we switch the bulb on we get out the light we want – and also produce heat that we don't need.

The electricity that makes both light and heat in the bulb is made in power stations. Power stations burn fuel such as oil or gas and use river water for cooling.

The fuel from the power stations needs to come from somewhere – usually from the ground. Mining or drilling for oil and gas also use up energy.

▼ ① **We live in a world where everything we do has connections worldwide.**

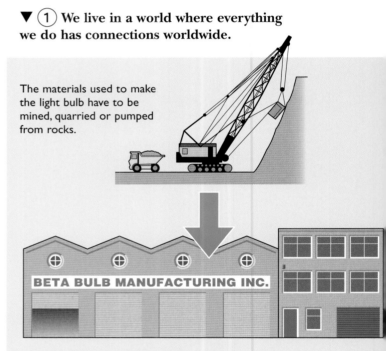

The materials used to make the light bulb have to be mined, quarried or pumped from rocks.

**BETA BULB MANUFACTURING INC.**

The bulb, the lampholder and the shade all have to be made, as does the wire that carries the electricity. So, in order to switch on the light at all, several materials have had to be used.

When we have finished with the bulb (or the lamp) we throw it away. This adds to the amount of waste we have to bury, unless we can recycle anything.

There is only so much oil, gas and coal. Eventually it will run out.

Power stations, just like cars and all other motors that use fuel, give out unwanted gases called **EXHAUST**. Some gases mix with the air, polluting it. Some gases affect our health. Other gases mix with water in the air and fall as **ACID RAIN** that kills trees and also affects life in rivers and lakes.

## It need not be a disaster

What we have seen is that the simple act of switching on a light causes a chain reaction of staggering complexity.

Just to get light, we have altered the ground, the air and water. So the challenge is how to get what we need with as little effect on the environment as possible. On the following pages, we shall see how to make the best of what we have.

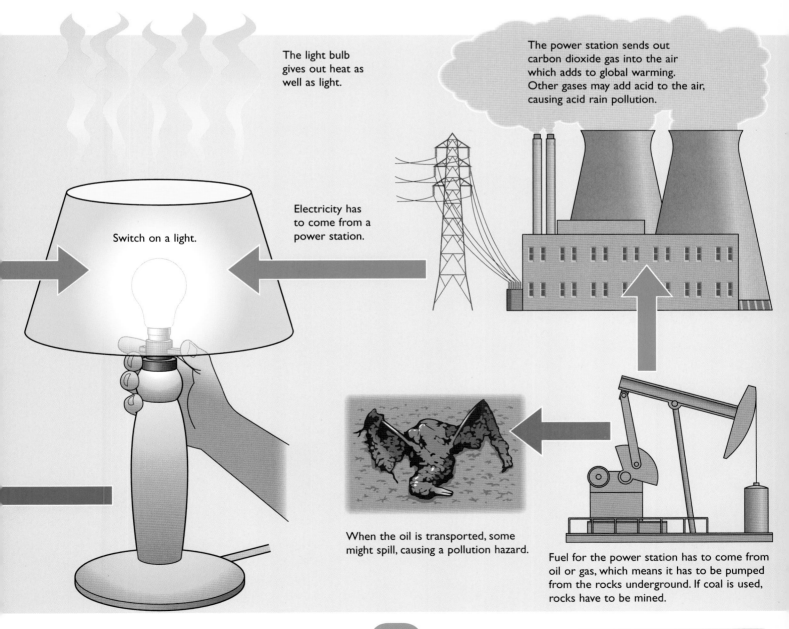

The light bulb gives out heat as well as light.

The power station sends out carbon dioxide gas into the air which adds to global warming. Other gases may add acid to the air, causing acid rain pollution.

Switch on a light.

Electricity has to come from a power station.

When the oil is transported, some might spill, causing a pollution hazard.

Fuel for the power station has to come from oil or gas, which means it has to be pumped from the rocks underground. If coal is used, rocks have to be mined.

# Saving energy at home

**Energy in the home costs money. But there are simple ways of saving energy and money. By doing this we are also helping the environment.**

We need to keep warm, cook our food and do many other things, But, as we have just seen, everything we do affects the world around us.

We can actually get light, heat and other kinds of energy in many ways. Some save more money – and thus more energy and more of the Earth's resources – than others.

## Cheaper lighting

In an ordinary bulb, electricity passes along a thin wire in the bulb, the wire gets hot and so gives out light. Only a tenth of the electricity used is given out as light.

Ordinary bulbs are therefore very wasteful ways of getting light.

Energy-saving bulbs (picture ①) are tiny fluorescent tubes. Inside them, electricity passes through a gas and this makes the outside of the tube glow. These tubes do not get hot, so nearly all the energy is given out as light. They also last much longer than bulbs and so they are better for the environment and save us money.

We can, of course, also save energy by switching off all electrical appliances when we don't need them.

## Cheaper heating

We heat homes with oil, coal, gas or electricity. We have to buy all of these. What we want is to heat the air in the rooms. But accidentally, we also heat the walls, the ceilings and the window panes, and much of this is lost. As a result, our heating bills can be far higher than they need to be.

▲ ① This 21 watt low-energy light bulb produces the same amount of light as a 100 watt light bulb for a fifth of the cost. It therefore saves burning oil, coal and gas and also helps keep air pollution under control.

To save money, we need to keep heat from leaking out through walls and ceilings (picture ②). The cheapest way to do this is to **INSULATE** walls and roofs. We do this by trapping air in foam insulation blocks or fibreglass. In windows we trap air inside double glazing.

We can also try to reduce draughts by using draught strips and better-fitting windows and doors.

Modern double-glazed doors can have a tight fit and use built-in draft-excluding strips.

▼ ② **Some ways of saving energy.**

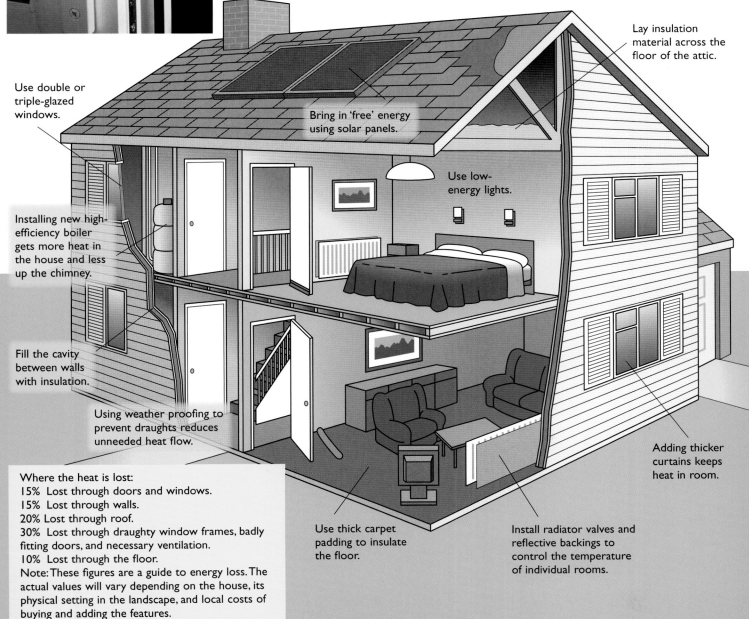

Lay insulation material across the floor of the attic.

Use double or triple-glazed windows.

Bring in 'free' energy using solar panels.

Use low-energy lights.

Installing new high-efficiency boiler gets more heat in the house and less up the chimney.

Fill the cavity between walls with insulation.

Using weather proofing to prevent draughts reduces unneeded heat flow.

Adding thicker curtains keeps heat in room.

Where the heat is lost:
15% Lost through doors and windows.
15% Lost through walls.
20% Lost through roof.
30% Lost through draughty window frames, badly fitting doors, and necessary ventilation.
10% Lost through the floor.
Note: These figures are a guide to energy loss. The actual values will vary depending on the house, its physical setting in the landscape, and local costs of buying and adding the features.

Use thick carpet padding to insulate the floor.

Install radiator valves and reflective backings to control the temperature of individual rooms.

# Saving energy, land and trees

**Not everyone can afford coal, oil and gas. Most of the world depends on wood for energy – and it is running out fast.**

We are so used to getting our energy from coal, oil and gas, that we can easily overlook the fact that most people in the world still do not have these kinds of energy at all.

In the countryside in poorer parts of the world, the only power most people get comes from wood they can collect themselves, or even the dried dung from their animals.

## Energy, soil and trees are linked

Poor people cannot afford to buy much energy. They must collect it from their fields.

Such people use tiny amounts of energy compared to ourselves and yet they have an energy problem far worse than us. The energy they use is also harmful to the environment.

▼ ① **How poor people can be forced to make the land poorer.**

Picture ① shows you the sort of problems that occur. Here you see a countryside area around a town in Africa. The people use fuelwood for cooking, heating and light.

They need to cut down trees to get the fuelwood, but the more trees they cut down, the fewer trees are left and the less energy they have.

The trees do not just give energy, they help hold the soil on hillsides, and the leaves even help feed their animals. With fewer trees, there is less food for animals, the bare soil gets washed away, and fewer crops can be grown. As a result people go hungry.

## Saving energy by planting

Picture ② shows how some people are overcoming their problem. They are planting new trees in places where they will best help protect the soil. They plant them across the slopes and at the edges of fields.

They are also planting at least as many trees as they cut down. In this way they will have a reliable supply of fuelwood and soil for growing their crops in the future. On steep slopes they have also made soil benches, called terraces, to keep the soil from washing away.

▼ ② Simple changes can make things better for people – and for the environment, too.

I have been shown how to make steps in the steep slopes that keep the soil from washing away.

I am now growing trees around my fields. They are a special kind that grow quickly and can be used for fuel.

I now have a better kind of stove that uses less fuel.

The land can now give food for more people.

Weblink: www.CurriculumVisions.com

# Saving water

**In the future, saving water will become more and more important. Much of what can be done is easy and just needs a little thought.**

In many parts of the world water is already in short supply. It also costs money to store water in reservoirs (picture ①) and to clean up dirty water. So is it possible to cut down on the amount we use and, if so, how can we do it?

## How farms can save water

Farms need lots of water during a dry summer. The simplest way of providing it is to flood the fields (picture ②). This is also the most wasteful way because a lot of the water **EVAPORATES** and is lost to the air.

▼ ① **Reservoirs save water, make electricity and stop floods, but they are costly to build. This is a dam on the Tennesse River.**

It saves huge amounts of water if farmers use a sprinkler (picture ③), and even more if they use pipes that drip water directly to plant roots.

## How water companies can save water

Water companies look after an enormous network of pipes. As pipes get old, many break or leak at the joints. Leaks waste billions of litres of water a day. By repairing leaks, water companies can play a major part in saving water.

Water companies take all of the polluted water from our sewers, clean it and put it back into rivers for **REUSE**. This is a vital way to save water.

▲ ② Flooding a farm with water is a wasteful way of using a valuable resource.

▲ ③ Using sprinklers that move across the fields is a much better way of using water.

## How we can save water

We can also help to save water. We can use toilets that flush with less water (picture ④) and we can take showers instead of baths. A shower (but not a power shower) uses a tenth of the water compared to a bath.

We can also use less water on our gardens and put it only on the flowers, not on the grass. A garden sprinkler uses about 15 litres of water a minute – about the same as a person in a poor country must carry to meet their daily needs.

These ways of saving mean that less money needs to be spent on cleaning water and on new reservoirs. The more we save, the less we get charged for our water and the less land we lose as reservoirs.

▲ ④ Using less water for flushing saves money. One way to save water is to put one or two bricks in the cistern.

Weblink: www.CurriculumVisions.com

# The waste we create

**When we have finished with something, we throw it away. This creates a great mixture of waste material.**

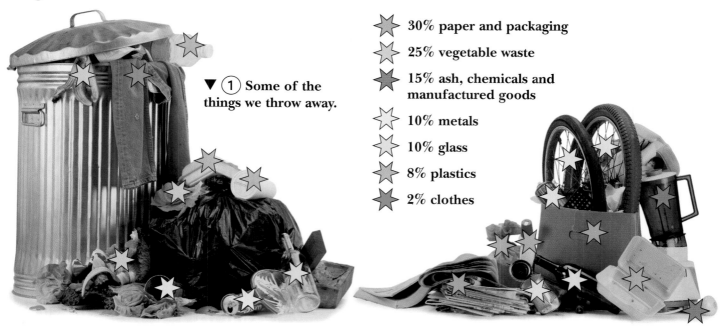

▼ ① Some of the things we throw away.

⭐ 30% paper and packaging

⭐ 25% vegetable waste

⭐ 15% ash, chemicals and manufactured goods

⭐ 10% metals

⭐ 10% glass

⭐ 8% plastics

⭐ 2% clothes

If you go into a supermarket and look around, what do you see? It's not food. What you see is packaging.

You might think of it as food because you know that inside the packaging is the food you want, but in order to get the food to you, the food makers have to put it into containers.

## Essential packaging

So why can't we just buy food unwrapped? This is, indeed, how we buy vegetables and fruit.

But this is the exception. Other fresh food, like meat, should not be handled. So it is packed – often in clear-sided plastic boxes.

Some kinds of food would be unsafe in a simple bag. Think about soup for example. A sharp pointed object would soon pierce the bag and create a mess. So strong cans or plastic tubs are needed.

Now think about **CEREALS**. These could be in floppy bags, but you wouldn't be able to get many stacked on a shelf without them falling on to the floor. You soon realise that we need boxes that have flat sides for these, and many other things.

## Dealing with packaging

So, packaging might appear wasteful when you go to throw it away (picture ①), but you can see that it actually performs a very useful range of jobs. We just have to make sure we recycle the packing afterwards and don't just throw it in the bin.

## Sorting our waste

Packaging only makes up part of our waste, of course.

Look at pictures ① and ② and you will see that what we throw away is made up of all kinds of things. Some is food, some is metal, some plastic, some glass, some pottery, some paper and so on.

How much of the things we use do we throw away? One way to find out about the waste we create is to do a home AUDIT.

▲ ② Sorting the waste into similar materials.

It is quite tricky to sort out waste when it gets to the rubbish tip, which is why we should try to sort some of it ourselves. Then it can be more easily reused, or recycled (picture ③).

RECYCLING CENTER

ALUMINUM CANS | PLASTIC BOTTLES 2-LITER ONLY | BROWN GLASS | CLEAR GLASS | GREEN GLASS

▶ ③ A recycling centre in a public place.

# What can we do with plastics?

Plastics may seem indestructible. But that does not mean we cannot make use of them time after time after time.

▲ ① Look on any beach and you will find that the majority of so-called flotsam – the material washed in with the waves – is made of plastic. This just shows how indestructible plastic is.

Whenever you look at rubbish that is left by the roadside or on a beach, you will often find that much of it is plastic.

About a fifth of all the rubbish people throw away is made of plastic (picture ①). So is there anything we can do with it?

## Sorting plastics

In fact, most common plastics are made of just a small range of materials. The trouble is that if these different plastics stay mixed up, they cannot be used for anything. This is why each type has now been given a recycle code (picture ②).

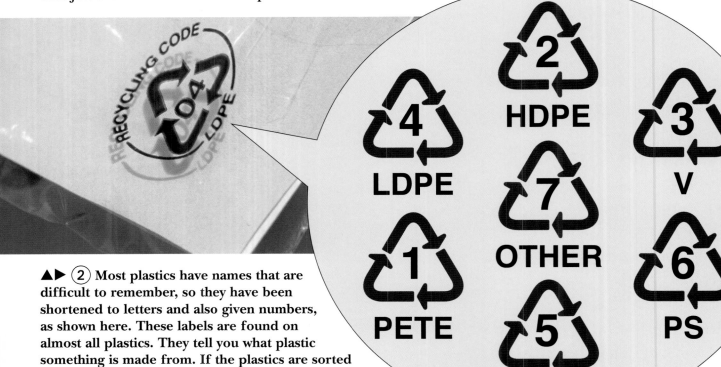

▲▶ ② Most plastics have names that are difficult to remember, so they have been shortened to letters and also given numbers, as shown here. These labels are found on almost all plastics. They tell you what plastic something is made from. If the plastics are sorted by number, many of them can be recycled.

RECYCLING CODE
04
LDPE

2 HDPE

4 LDPE

3 V

1 PETE

7 OTHER

6 PS

5 PP

▲ ③ Polystyrene (PS) makes a surprising number of things around us, from disposable cups (top right) and CD cases (top left) to plastic knives and forks. It can easily be recycled if we sort it from other rubbish.

If you look on most plastic objects you should find the code (picture ③). The only things that don't have codes tend to be plastic sheet, such as plastic bags and carrier bags, but most of these are made of either HDPE or LDPE plastic. Most of numbers 1 to 6 can be melted down and used again – recycled. So we can help by sorting them.

## Surprising new uses

Many plastics are coloured. This means that we have to use the recycled plastic in places where this doesn't matter. Here are some examples.

Where do you think plastic flower pots come from? Many of them were once plastic bags that were returned to the supermarket. They have been melted down, and a dark brown or black colour added to hide the colours the bags may have had before.

Where do you think traffic cones come from? Many of them are recycled plastic bottles with a strong colour added (picture ④).

When plastics cannot be sorted out, all is not lost. They can be ground to a powder, fused together and made into slabs of plastic which are used, for example, to make weatherproof park benches!

▶ ④ Traffic cones: recycled plastic bottles.

# Making use of paper

We use paper as packaging, newspaper and books. If we can help to recycle it, then fewer forests need be cut down.

▲ ① Books that have had their cardboard covers removed ready to be recycled.

Enormous amounts of money are spent on dealing with our paper rubbish. It is expensive to pick up and to sort out for recycling (picture ①). Even what is left over is expensive to deal with. This is because it still has to be burnt or buried in a landfill site.

The material that gets burnt or buried cannot be used again. Yet money was spent on cutting down trees and making the paper in the first place.

This is all very inefficient, so it makes environmental sense and saves money to sort as much as we can and reuse it.

## What is paper?

Paper is made of long, thin fibres of plant material all mashed together.

Most of the fibres come from wood. Paper also has glue and ink on it and many papers also contain white clay to give the paper a smoother finish.

## Recycling paper

Because printed paper contains many materials, you cannot easily recycle waste paper to make higher quality paper. You need to look for different uses where quality is less important.

There are many uses for recycled paper – especially in packaging, toilet paper and home insulation (picture ②). Look at different packages. Can you see which cereal cartons, for example, are made from recycled materials? If they are grey on the inside they are probably made from recycled paper.

## Why we need to recycle paper

Why don't we leave it to the dustman to sort out the paper for us? Why should we sort it and put it out separately?

The answer is that paper is very difficult to sort out from other waste, especially when it gets wet. If you take a piece of paper and leave it out in the rain, it goes soggy. When you pull on it, it tears. It has very little strength when wet.

Much of our dustbin waste is made of wet materials such as vegetable peelings and tea bags, and these make the paper in a dustbin wet and dirty. Then it cannot be separated and recycled.

The only people who can easily make sure that paper is given to the dustman in dry condition are ourselves. Which is why we need to sort paper at home. Then it can be recycled (picture ③).

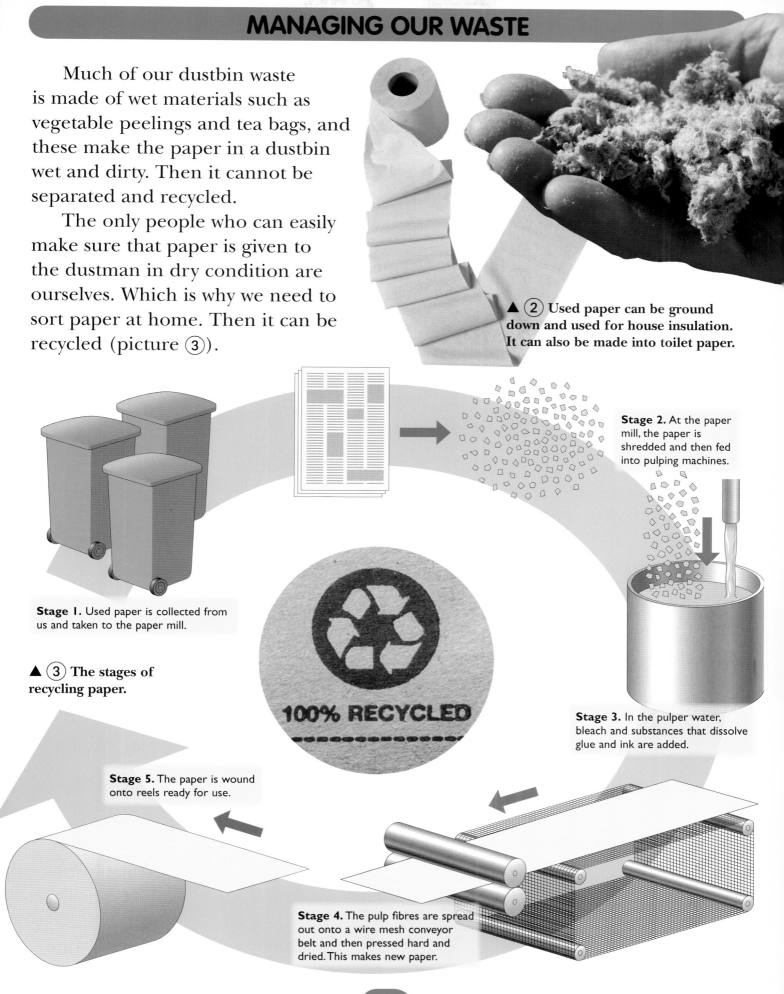

▲ ② Used paper can be ground down and used for house insulation. It can also be made into toilet paper.

**Stage 1.** Used paper is collected from us and taken to the paper mill.

▲ ③ The stages of recycling paper.

**Stage 2.** At the paper mill, the paper is shredded and then fed into pulping machines.

**Stage 3.** In the pulper water, bleach and substances that dissolve glue and ink are added.

100% RECYCLED

**Stage 5.** The paper is wound onto reels ready for use.

**Stage 4.** The pulp fibres are spread out onto a wire mesh conveyor belt and then pressed hard and dried. This makes new paper.

Weblink: www.CurriculumVisions.com

# Environmentally friendly materials

**By making environmentally friendly materials we can help preserve the Earth.**

Think of some of the things we use just once and then throw away: packaging, picnic knives, forks and spoons, hamburger boxes, baby nappies and so on. The list seems endless.

If they are made of plastic they will never rot away and so they are not at all environmentally friendly. If we burned them, then they would release gases and heat into the air, causing pollution and global warming. So that is not environmentally friendly either.

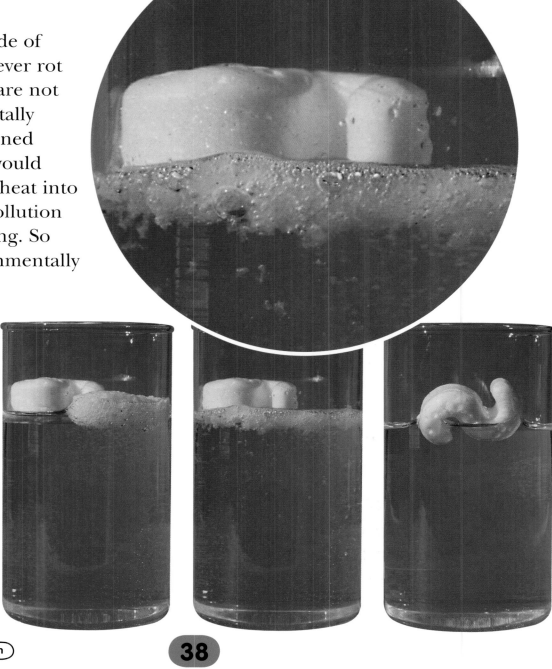

▶ ① **Starch packaging chips dissolve in a few minutes while plastic (polystyrene) packaging chips do not break down at all.**

You can tell which kind you have because starch packaging chips have a slight food-like smell, unlike the plastic which has no smell.

▲ ② These plant-protecting sheets are only needed for a few weeks to protect crops from frost. If made of a starch-based material they will rot away on their own.

## Think environment

Paper and plastic packaging, for example, can be environmentally friendly if they can be recycled. The trouble is that these things usually can't be recycled because they are mixed in with the rest of our rubbish.

It would be better if some types of packaging, for example carrier bags or packaging pellets, could rot away entirely and not leave anything behind.

## Make it rot

We don't want packaging to rot while we are using it. Instead, we want it to behave normally while it is dry, then dissolve when it gets wet, for example, when it is buried in a rubbish tip.

It is now possible to use a substance found in plants to make materials that look like plastic. This substance is called STARCH, and it is the white liquid you find in potatoes, rice and many other plants.

When packaging pellets are kept dry there is no difference between starch pellets and plastic pellets. But when they are put in the ground, the starch dissolves quickly (picture ①). Plastic would stay in the ground for ever.

Starch can also be made to dissolve at different rates. For example, on a farm, protective sheets can be used that will dissolve as plants grow (picture ②).

# Water pollution

**There are many causes of water pollution. Some are easier to control than others.**

When people say that water is 'dirty', they don't just mean that it contains materials like soil. They may also mean that it contains chemicals, such as oil and detergents, or **GERMS** that make it unhealthy. A better word for all kinds of 'dirty' water is **POLLUTED WATER** (picture ①). Human waste in water is also called **SEWAGE**.

## Pollution

All water contains a few tiny pieces of soil and some harmless invisible chemicals.

Water is polluted when too much soil and unhealthy substances get into the water.

This is still a big problem in many rivers where the river is used as a cheap form of **SEWER** or dumping ground.

▼ ① **Some of the sources of water pollution.**

### This kind of pollution is hard to control

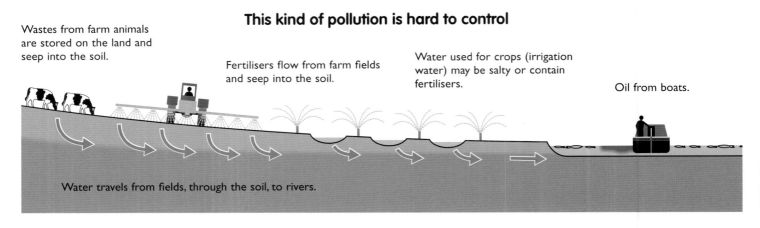

Wastes from farm animals are stored on the land and seep into the soil.

Fertilisers flow from farm fields and seep into the soil.

Water used for crops (irrigation water) may be salty or contain fertilisers.

Oil from boats.

Water travels from fields, through the soil, to rivers.

### This kind of pollution is easier to control

Waste from home toilets and sinks will cause pollution if it goes straight into rivers. Instead, it is usually collected in pipes and taken to sewage works. In country areas, without mains pipes, each house has its own underground septic tank. From time to time, the sewage is collected and taken to a sewage works.

Wastes from factories are often highly polluted and need to be treated by special means. This is often done on the factory premises.

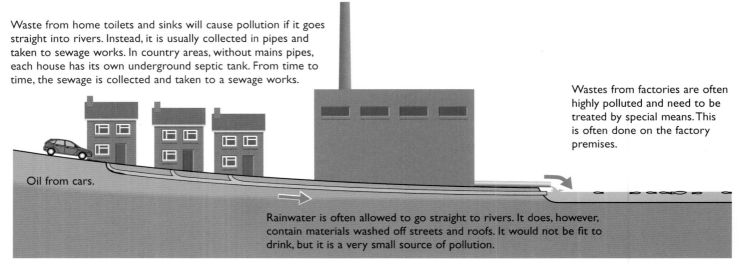

Oil from cars.

Rainwater is often allowed to go straight to rivers. It does, however, contain materials washed off streets and roofs. It would not be fit to drink, but it is a very small source of pollution.

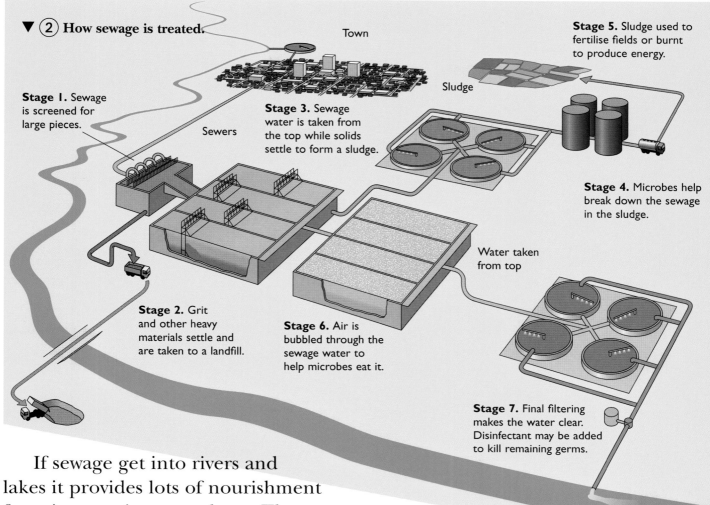

▼ ② How sewage is treated.

Town

**Stage 5.** Sludge used to fertilise fields or burnt to produce energy.

Sludge

**Stage 1.** Sewage is screened for large pieces.

Sewers

**Stage 3.** Sewage water is taken from the top while solids settle to form a sludge.

**Stage 4.** Microbes help break down the sewage in the sludge.

Water taken from top

**Stage 2.** Grit and other heavy materials settle and are taken to a landfill.

**Stage 6.** Air is bubbled through the sewage water to help microbes eat it.

**Stage 7.** Final filtering makes the water clear. Disinfectant may be added to kill remaining germs.

If sewage get into rivers and lakes it provides lots of nourishment for microscopic water plants. These grow and take oxygen from the water. As a result the water turns green and there is not enough oxygen left for good **MICROBES** to clean the water.

In some countries rivers also become polluted by factory wastes containing harmful chemicals.

## How sewage is cleaned

If you put a small amount of sewage into a large amount of water (**DILUTION**), then the natural microbes in the water will eat the sewage and clean up the water naturally (the solution!). They will not, however, get rid of the solid materials.

So before you can begin to let microbes do their work, all of the solids must be filtered out (picture ② **stage 2**).

The water now contains only human waste and chemicals. Some settles (**stage 3**) and makes sludge which can then be spread on farmland as a fertiliser (**stage 5**).

Air is bubbled through the remaining water to help microbes break down the sewage into gases and water (**stage 6**). Any remaining germs can then be killed with a disinfectant like chlorine (**stage 7**).

## The Exxon Valdez disaster

On March 24, 1989 the oil tanker Exxon Valdez ran aground in Prince William Sound, Alaska, spilling an estimated 50 million litres of crude oil across 2,100 kilometres of coastline.

While much of the polluted coast now appears to have recovered, pockets of crude oil remain in some places, and there is evidence that some damage is still continuing over a decade later.

▲ ① Cleanup workers spray oiled rocks with high pressure hoses.

# Oil pollution

**We carry vast amounts of oil overland in pipes and across seas in tankers. As a result, when oil spills it can have enormous effects on the environment.**

We get oil from the ground. We use it to heat our homes, cook our food, power our machines, make plastics, medicines and many other things.

We need to get it from where it is pumped out of the ground to where we use it. This is done by pipelines and oil tankers.

## Oil spills and oil dumping

Pipelines can break and spill oil over the land. But far worse, oil tankers can be wrecked by storms and by collisions (picture ① and 'The Exxon Valdez disaster'). Then oil will spill into the sea causing enormous oil pollution.

Accidental spills cause bad pollution (picture ②), but most oil gets into the sea when ships clean out their holds (picture ③).

Whatever the cause, some oil floats and is carried with ocean currents onto beaches where it kills coastal birds and animals (picture ④).

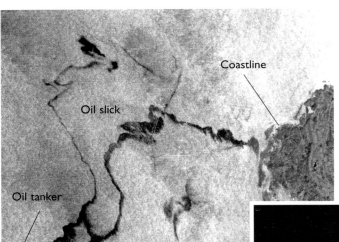

Coastline

Oil slick

Oil tanker

▲▶ ② The satellite picture above shows an oil slick spreading hundreds of kilometres from a sunken ship to the beaches of a distant coast (land in green). Surface oil can be trapped using floating booms (right).

► ③ **The kinds of pollution caused by misusing oil.**

Tanker accidents 12%

Other 9%

Cleaning tankers at sea 33%

Factory discharges and oil running into city drains 37%

Spills during production of oil 2%

Natural sources 7%

Some oil sinks and kills animals on the sea bed.

If we are careless with the oil we use on land, it spills onto roads and gets into rivers where it can cause more destruction (picture ⑤).

We need oil, but we can reduce the destruction oil spills cause if we take steps to prevent them.

▲ ④ Workers struggling to clean up an oil spill on a beach.

► ⑤ Local oil spills on land can be very damaging but they are easier to trap than spills on a beach.

# Air pollution

**When we release gases and tiny bits of soot into the air we can cause great damage over a wide area.**

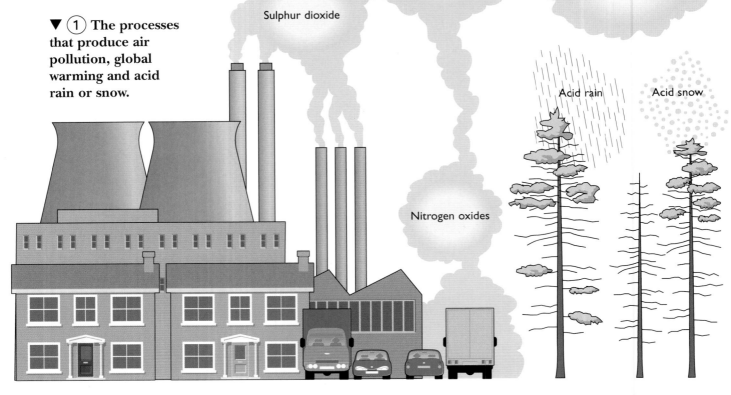

▼ ① The processes that produce air pollution, global warming and acid rain or snow.

Sulphur dioxide

Gases are converted into acids when they react and dissolve in water.

Amongst other acids, sulphuric acid and nitric acid are produced.

Acid rain

Acid snow

Nitrogen oxides

Do you think the air you breathe is fresh and clean? If you do, then you need to think again.

Just like water can look clean and still contain unseen harmful things, so the air can seem clean but contain all kinds of harmful gases and dirt, some that we can see, and many we cannot.

## The six common pollutants

The air is a mixture of gases. Some are harmful but most are not. We are now increasing the amount of harmful gases in the air. This is **AIR POLLUTION** (picture ①).

The six most common air pollutants are five gases – ozone, lead, sulphur dioxide (picture ②), nitrogen dioxide (picture ③), carbon monoxide – and tiny bits of dirt (soot and dust).

▶ ② Where sulphur gases come from.

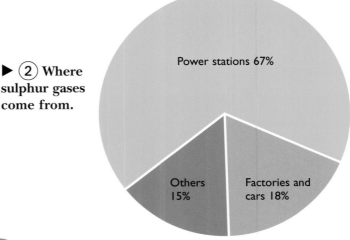

Power stations 67%

Others 15%

Factories and cars 18%

▶ ④ The 'hole' in the ozone layer over the Arctic and Antarctic (shown here by the darker blues) has been produced by pollution. Less ozone means that higher levels of harmful ultraviolet light can pass through the atmosphere. This increases the risk of skin cancers. Those living nearer the poles and those who sunbathe a lot are most at risk.

## Where air pollution comes from

Air pollution comes from many different sources. Factories (including metal works and chemical works) and power stations may give out lots of pollution. If you live near one of them, you probably get more pollution than someone living far away.

Much of this pollution can be screened out – at a price.

But a large proportion of pollution comes from cars, buses, planes, trucks and trains. So if you live in a city or next to a main road, the chances are your air will be more polluted than if you live in the countryside.

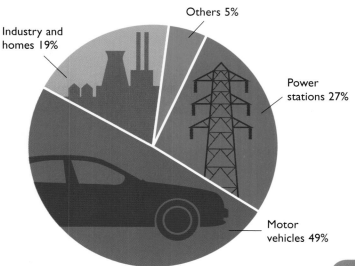

▼ ③ Where nitrogen gases come from.

Others 5%

Industry and homes 19%

Power stations 27%

Motor vehicles 49%

## Haze

On calm days in summer or winter, the air gradually becomes more and more hazy. Most of this **HAZE** is not natural. It is the steady build-up of pollution in the air.

Modern air pollution has cut down how far we can see by a third to a half compared to what it would be like if there were no pollution at all. When it rains, most of this pollution is washed out, which is why you can see farther after rain.

## What can pollution do?

Some of the pollutants have been linked to serious health problems and environmental damage: sore eyes and an irritated throat, breathing illnesses such as asthma, and **ACID RAIN** that can kill trees and also fish in lakes and rivers (see picture ②, page 4).

Pollution can also destroy the protective layer of ozone high in the air (picture ④).

# Glossary

**ACID RAIN** Rain which has been contaminated by dissolving gases from the air. The gases make the rain acid. This can kill plants and water life.

**AIR POLLUTION** Air which contains unnaturally large amounts of gases and dirt that have been released by vehicles, power stations and factories.

**ANNUAL** A plant which completes its life from sprouting seed, through flowering, making new seeds and dying all in a single year.

**AUDIT** A way of counting up all of the uses to find out what is really going on.

**BALANCE OF NATURE** The way that all living things form part of food chains which keep their numbers in check, so that nothing increases too much and wipes out all of the others.

**CARNIVORE** A hunting animal that eats only meat.

**CEREAL** The seeds of many grasses that we use for food.

**CONSERVE** To keep safely so that nothing becomes endangered or goes extinct through the carelessness of people's actions.

**CONSUME, CONSUMER** To make use of or use up.

**CROP** A plant that we grow in fields and which is used for food (e.g. wheat) or to make things such as fabrics (e.g. cotton).

**DILUTE/DILUTION** To make a solution of something weaker, often by adding water.

**ENDANGERED** A living thing whose numbers are falling rapidly and which, if nothing is done, may soon become extinct.

**EROSION** The wearing away of the land, usually by heavy rain or wind.

**EVAPORATE** The change of water from liquid to vapour. When water evaporates from a reservoir the level of water falls.

**EXHAUST** The burnt gases that come from an engine. These gases often combine with the air to make new irritating or harmful gases.

**EXTINCT** A group of living things that can no longer be found alive in the world today, for example, dinosaurs.

**FERTILE** A soil that contains all of the nourishment it needs to allow plants to grow healthily.

**FOOD CHAIN** A naturally-linked collection of living things, each one, except the top one, being food for another. The bottom of the food chain normally starts with plants, which are food for grazing animals. These are food for hunters. Plants, grazing and hunting animals make up a food chain.

**FOSSIL** The remains of a former living thing that has become preserved in rocks.

**FOSSIL FUEL** A fuel produced from plants or animals long ago that is found in the Earth's crust. The main fossil fuels are coal, gas and oil.

**GAME PARK** An area of wilderness in which animals roam freely and in which there are a large number of large animals. Game animals are those which are often shot by human hunters for sport.

**GERMS** Very small pieces of living matter that can develop and cause disease. They include bacteria and viruses.

**GLOBAL WARMING** The gradual warming of the world's air as a result of the heat we are pumping into it by burning fuels.

**HABITAT** A place in which a living thing can live out its life. A rock pool, a pond and a river are all different kinds of habitat.

**HAZE** Poor visibility that often occurs on sunny days. It is caused by the build-up of pollution in the air. Haze disappears after rain washes the pollutants from the air.

**HEDGE** A boundary made from natural shrubs and trees that are cut back each year to keep them bushy.

**HERBACEOUS PLANT** Leafy plants with no woody stem.

**ICE AGE** The time, some tens of thousands of years ago, when the world became a much colder place and ice sheets spread out from mountains and the poles.

**INSULATE** To stop heat from moving. Air is one of the best insulators.

**MAMMAL** An animal that provides milk for its babies.

**MICROBE** A tiny living thing, such as a bacterium.

**MULCH** A surface covering of material designed to prevent water being lost from soil and weeds growing up. It can be made from dead plant remains, bark chippings and many other materials.

**OIL POLLUTION** Water that has been contaminated with oil. Although oil and water do not mix, it can be very difficult to separate spilled oil from water and as a result oil pollution can spread widely.

**ORGANIC FARMING** A way of growing crops and rearing animals that uses natural means to control pests and return nourishment to the soil.

**PERENNIAL** A plant which grows a bit more each year and has a lifespan of several years. Trees are the longest-living perennial plants, sometimes living for thousands of years.

**PEST** A living thing that occurs in such numbers that it becomes a nuisance to people.

**PLANTATION** A very large area of farm or forest land that grows just one crop.

**POACHER** A person who kills wildlife (mostly game) without the permission of the landowner.

**POLLEN** The tiny yellow grains produced by flowers and which are carried by the insects or the wind to other flowers so that seeds can be produced.

**POLLUTE** To add harmful substances to air, soil or water.

**POLLUTED WATER** Water which contains a large amount of harmful chemicals or germs.

**RECYCLE** To make use of a material more than once.

**REPTILE** A cold-blooded animal that moves on the ground like a snake or moves on short legs like a lizard.

**RESOURCES** Anything that we make use of to make things we want.

**REUSE** To make use of a manufactured object more than once.

**RODENT** A small mammal with teeth designed for gnawing.

**SCRUB** A kind of wilderness in which only herbs and shrubs grow.

**SEWAGE** The waste material that we produce from our sinks and toilets.

**SEWER** A large pipe designed to carry sewage.

**SHRUB** A plant of a few metres high and which has a woody stem.

**SPECIES** A group of living things that can breed together.

**STARCH** A white substance made by plants and which can be made into a substance like plastic, or into an adhesive or can be eaten as a source of energy.

**STEWARDSHIP** The business of looking after the environment so that all living things get a fair chance to survive and are not driven to extinction by people.

**WEEDS** Any plant that has grown unwanted in a cultivated plot like a garden or field.

**WILDERNESS** An area in which people have not played an important part.

▲ **Poor people recycling waste for a living, Mexico City.**

# Index

acid rain  4, 23, 25, 44, 45, 46
acid snow  44
air pollution  4, 25, 26, 38, 44–45, 46
animal waste  18, 19, 28, 40
animals  4, 6, 7, 8–9, 10–11, 12, 13, 15, 16, 17, 18, 19, 20, 21, 28, 29, 40, 42, 43
annual  17, 46
audit  33, 46

balance (of nature)  6, 7, 15, 18, 20, 46
birds  6, 7, 12, 13, 15, 16, 17, 18, 20, 21, 42

carbon dioxide  23, 25
carbon monoxide  44
carnivores  10, 46
cereal  18, 32, 36, 46
chemicals  19, 22, 32, 40, 41, 45
clay  22, 23, 36
coal  4, 22, 25, 26, 28
conserve/conservation  5, 11, 46
consume/consumer  22–23, 24–25, 26–27, 28–29, 30–31, 46
crops  4, 6, 11, 18, 19, 29, 39, 40, 46

dinosaurs  6
dodo  7
double glazing  27

ecosystem  11
ecotourism  11
electricity  4, 22, 23, 24, 25, 26, 30
elephants  8, 9
endangered animals  8–9, 46
endangered forests  12–13, 46
energy  22, 23, 24, 26–27, 28–29, 41
energy-saving initiatives  22, 26–27, 28–29
environment, damaging our  4, 12–13, 14, 18, 20, 25, 28–29, 38, 42–43, 44–45
environment, improving our  5, 13, 15, 16–17, 19, 20, 21, 26–27, 29, 38–39
environmentally friendly materials  38–39
erosion  19, 28, 29, 46
Ethiopian wolf  10
evaporate/evaporation  30, 46
exhaust gases  25, 46
extinct/extinction  6–7, 9, 10, 46

factory waste  40, 41, 43, 45
farming  10, 11, 12, 14–15, 18–19, 28, 29, 30, 31, 39, 40, 41
fertiliser  14, 18, 40, 41
fish  4, 20, 21, 45

food chain  11, 46
forest  4, 6, 12–13, 14, 23, 36
fossil fuels  22. *See also* coal, gas, oil
fossils  6, 46
fuels  4, 11, 22, 24–25, 26, 28–29
fuelwood  28, 29

game park  11, 46
garden  16–17, 23, 31
gas  23, 24, 25, 26, 28, 38, 41, 44–45
germs  40, 41, 46
glass  23, 24, 32, 33
global warming  23, 25, 38, 44, 46

habitat  5, 11, 18, 46
haze  45, 46
hedge  17, 18, 19, 46
home energy  26–27
human waste  40, 41
hunters  8, 9, 10, 11, 12, 19, 21

Ice Age  13, 46
insulate/insulation  27, 36, 37, 46
ivory  8, 9, 11

light bulbs  24–25, 26, 27

mammal  17, 46
manure  19
metal  22, 24, 32, 33, 45
microbes  41, 46
mulch  19, 46

national park  5, 9, 11, 15
natural cycle  13, 19
natural environment  12, 13, 14–15, 18, 20, 21. *See also* wilderness
nitrogen gases  44, 45
nourishment  13, 18, 19, 41

oil  4, 22, 23, 24, 25, 26, 28, 40, 42–43
oil pollution  40, 42–43, 46
organic farming  18–19, 46
oxygen  13, 41
ozone  44, 45
ozone layer  45

packaging  32, 33, 36, 38–39
paper  12, 32, 33, 36–37
peat  23
perennial  17, 47
pests  19, 47
petrol  22
plantation  12–13, 47
plants  7, 12, 13, 15, 16, 17, 18, 19, 20, 21, 39, 41
plastic (material)  22, 23, 24, 32, 33, 34–35, 38–39
poacher  9, 11, 47
pollute/pollution  4, 5, 18, 20, 21, 23, 25, 26, 30, 38, 40–41, 42–43, 44–45, 47
polystyrene  22, 35, 38
power station  24, 25, 44, 45

quarries  14, 15, 23, 24
recycling centre  33
recycling metal  22, 32, 33
recycling paper/cardboard  22, 32, 33, 36–37
recycling nourishment  18
recycling plastic  22, 32, 33, 34–35, 39
recycling rubbish  22, 23, 24, 32–33, 36–37, 39
reptile  15, 47
reservoir  30, 31
resources  22–23, 24–25, 26–27, 28–29, 30–31, 47
reuse  23, 33, 36, 47
rhinoceros  9
rivers  4, 20–21, 24, 25, 30, 40–41, 43, 45
rodent  15, 47
rubbish  23, 32–33, 34, 35, 36, 39, 41

scrub  19, 47
sewage  30, 40–41, 47
sewage works  30, 40–41
sewer  30, 40, 41, 47
showers  31
shrubs  16, 17, 47
soil  13, 14, 18, 19, 21, 23, 28, 29, 40
solar panels  27
species  4, 6, 8, 9, 13, 20, 47
sprinklers  30, 31
starch  38, 39, 47
stewardship  5, 20, 47
sulphur gases  44

toilets  31, 40
tourism  11
trees  4, 7, 12, 13, 14, 17, 18, 20, 22, 23, 25, 28, 29, 36, 45

waste  23, 32–33, 34–35, 36–37, 38–39, 40
waste paper  32, 33, 36–37
water  4, 10, 18, 20, 21, 25, 30–31, 37, 40–41, 44
water pollution (polluted water)  4, 20, 21, 30, 40–41, 47
water-saving initiatives  30–31, 41
weeds  19, 20, 21, 47
whale  8, 9
wilderness  11, 14–15, 16, 47
wolf  10, 11
wood (material)  12, 14, 15, 17, 22, 23, 28, 29, 36
woodland  12, 13, 18. *See also* forest